How To Draw Realistic Skulls Volume 6

Simple Guide to Drawing Skulls

How to Draw Skulls

By : Gala Publication

Published By :

Gala Publication

© Copyright 2015 – Gala Publication

ISBN-13: **978-1522785859**
ISBN-10: **152278585X**

ALL RIGHTS RESERVED. No part of this publication may be reproduced or transmitted in any form whatsoever, electronic, or mechanical, including photocopying, recording, or by any informational storage or retrieval system without express written, dated and signed permission from the author.

Table of Contents

Learn To Draw Skull 6 Characters: ....

Learn To Draw Army Skull ....

Learn To Draw Cow Skull..

Learn To Draw Fiery Skull..

Learn To Draw Human Skull....................................

Learn To Draw Sonics Skull......................................

Learn To Draw Spongebobs Skull ....

ARMY SKULL

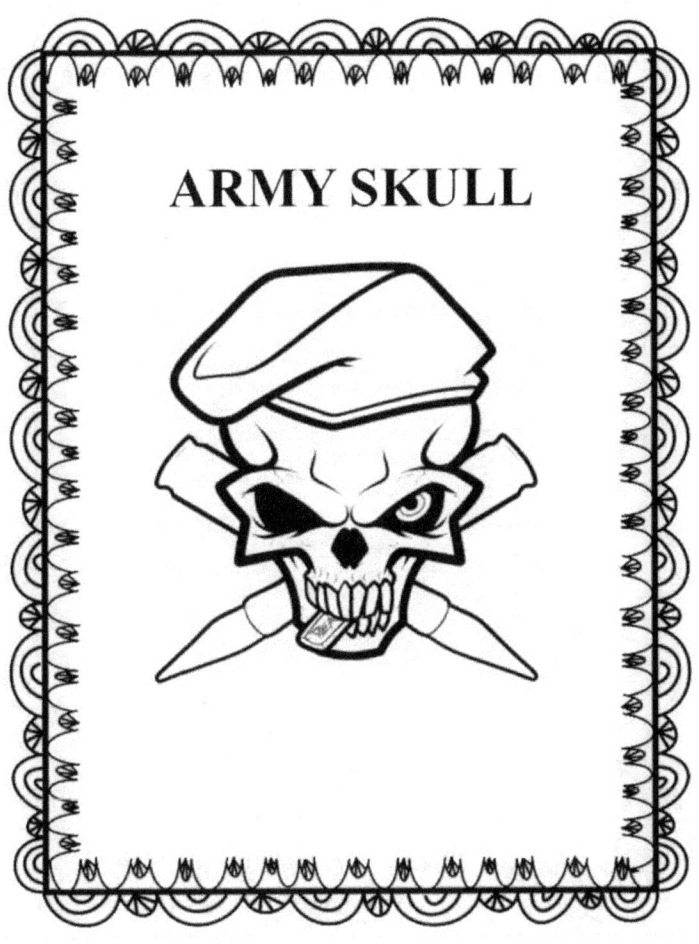

STEP 1

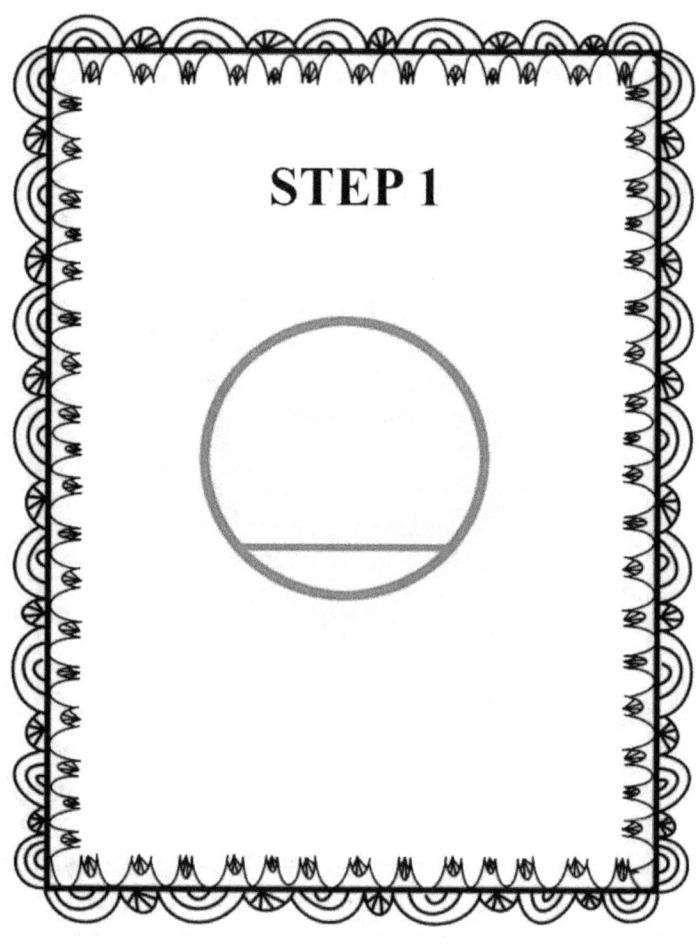

STEP 2

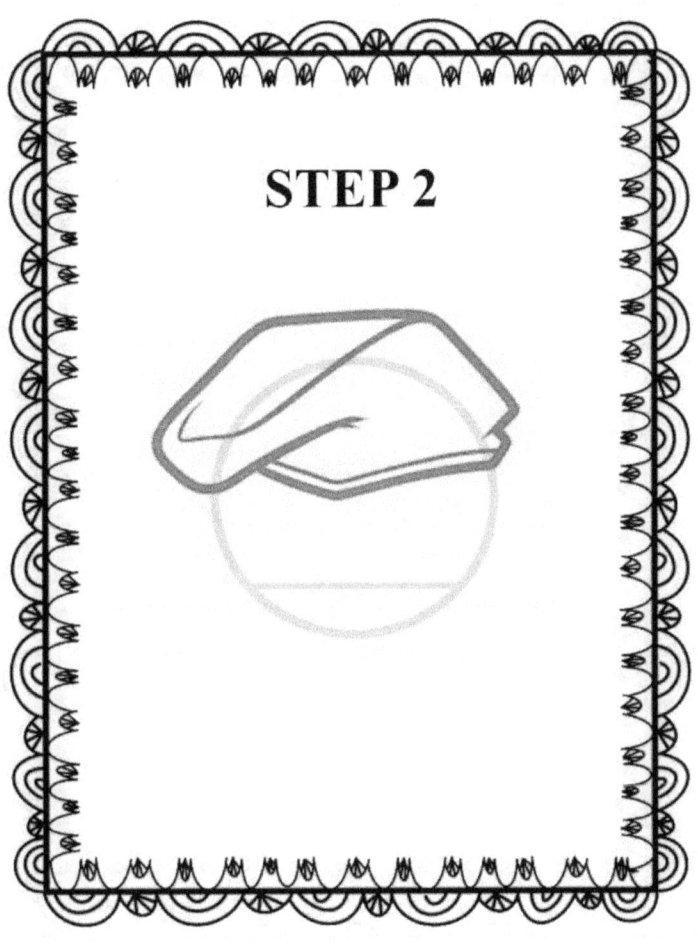

STEP 3

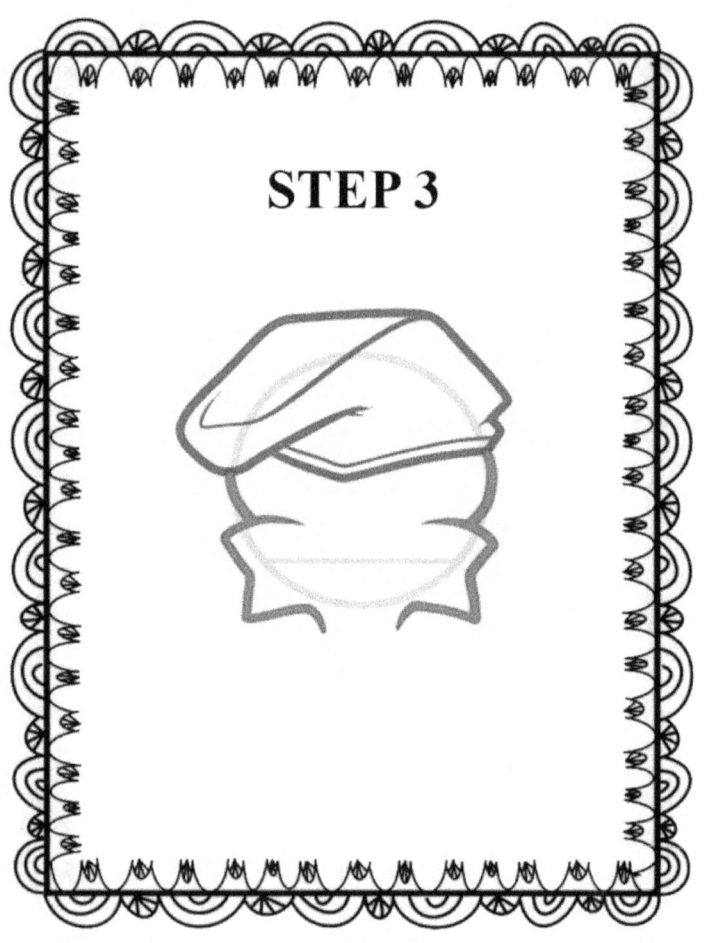

STEP 4

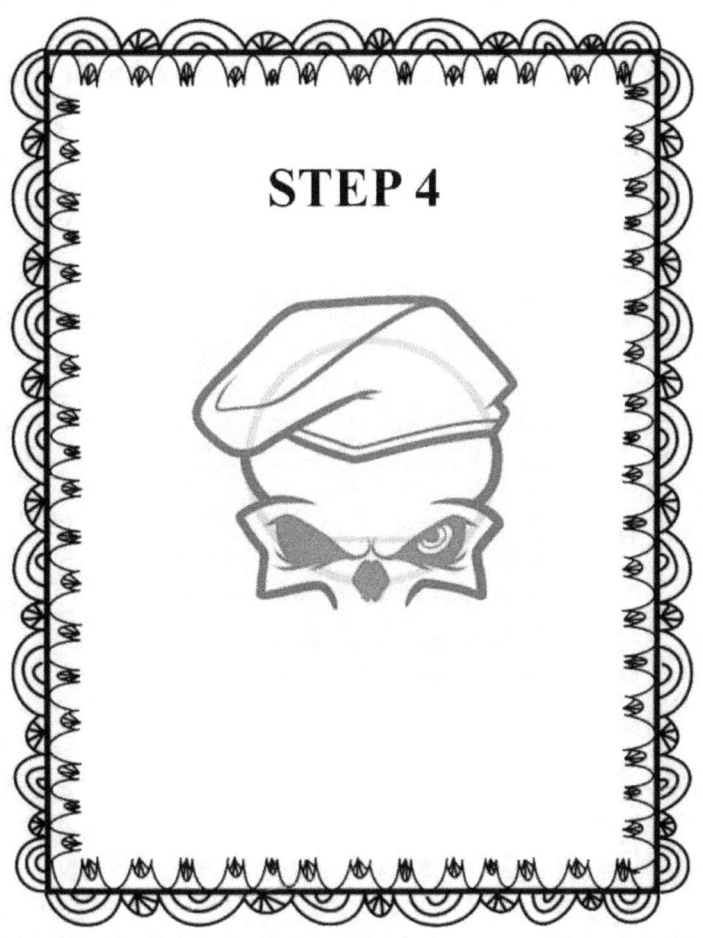

STEP 5

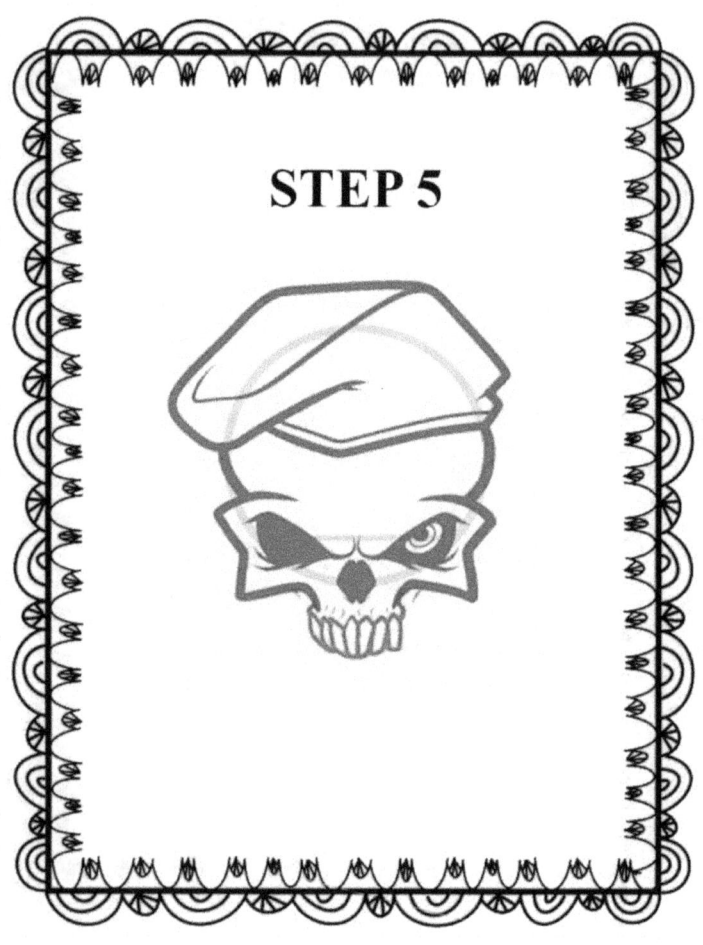

STEP 6

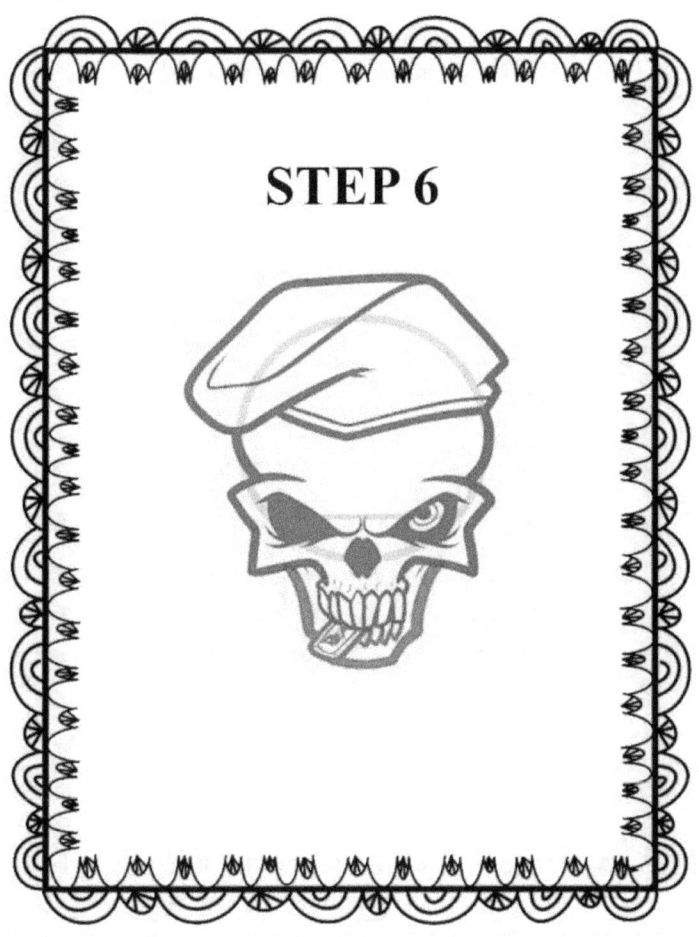

STEP 7

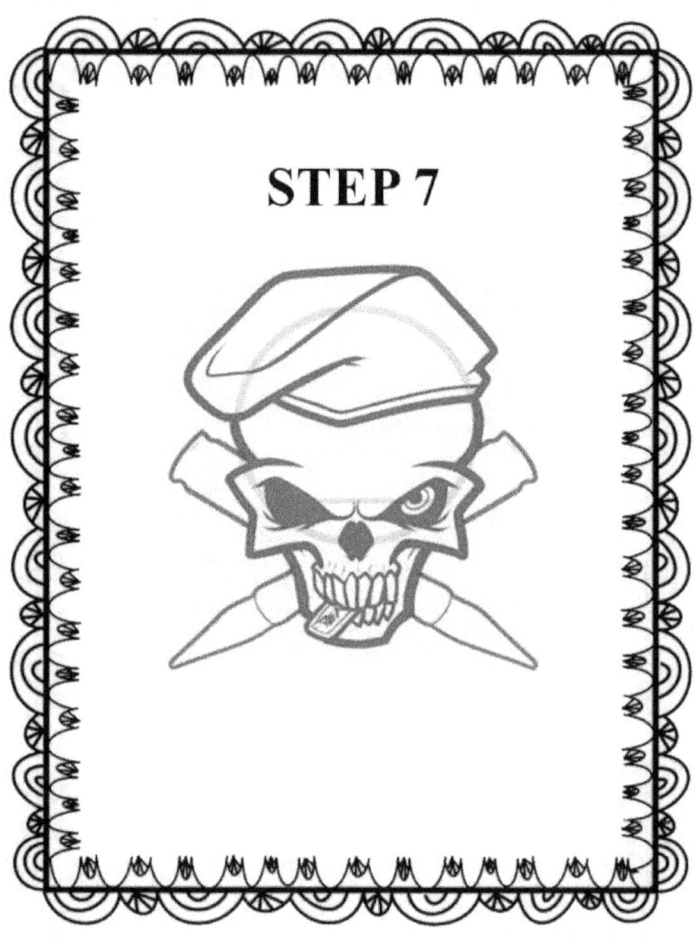

STEP 8

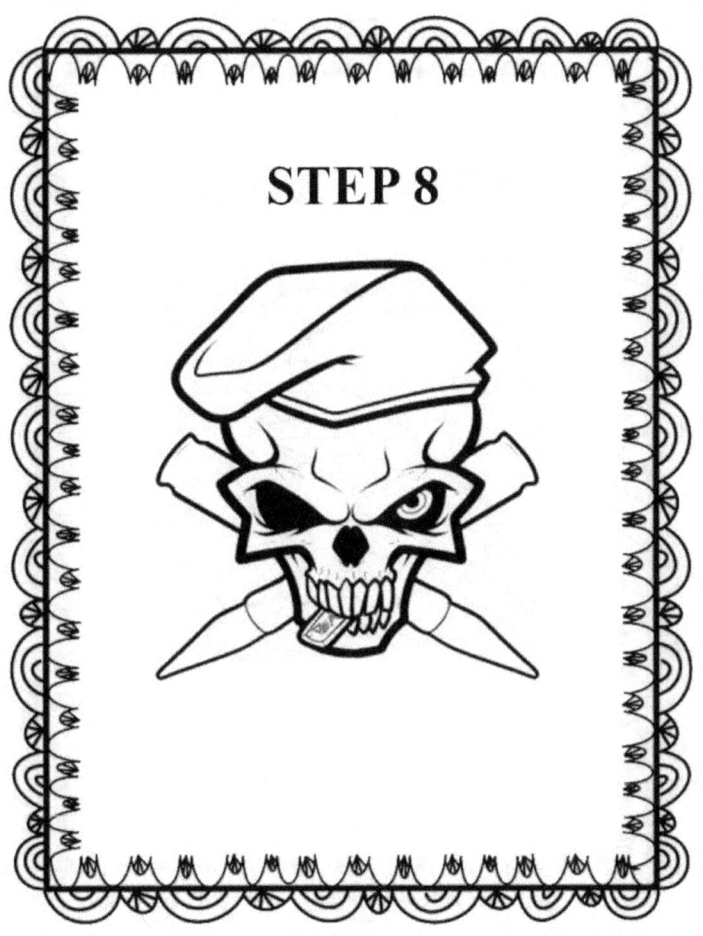

COW SKULL

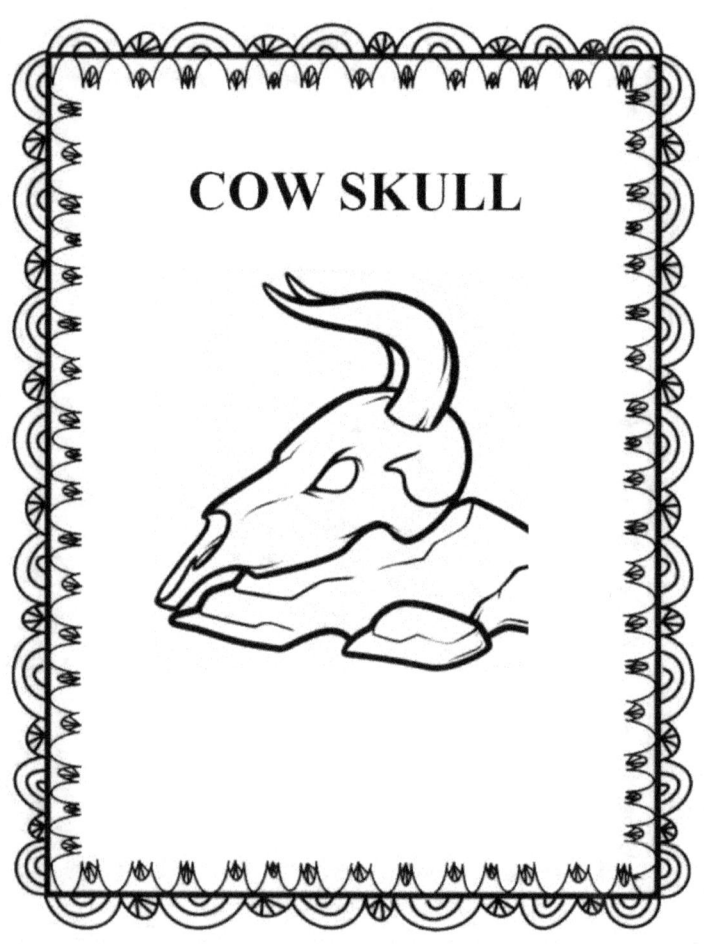

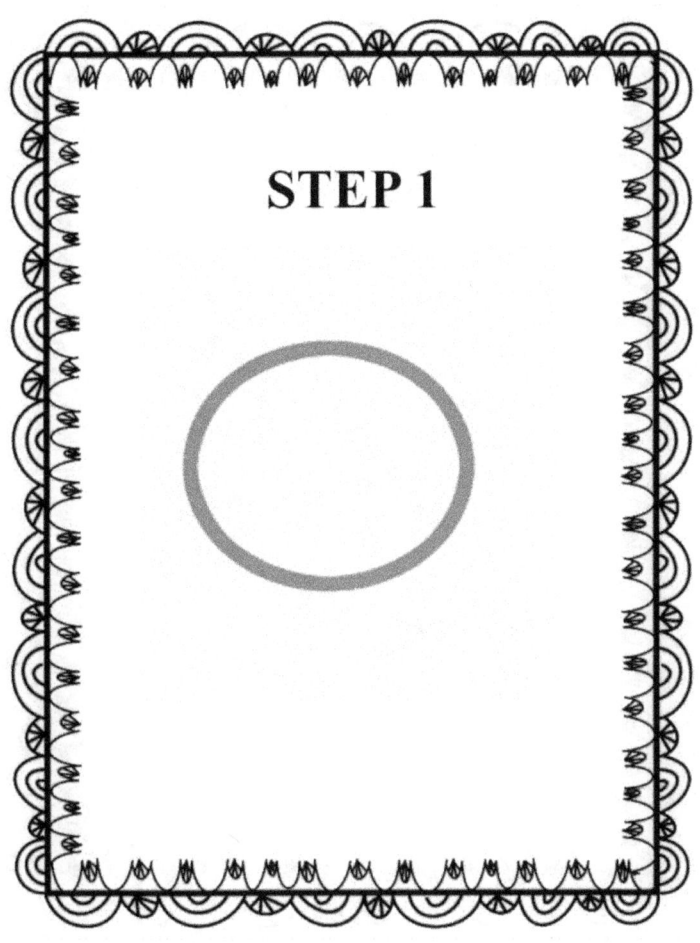

STEP 1

STEP 2

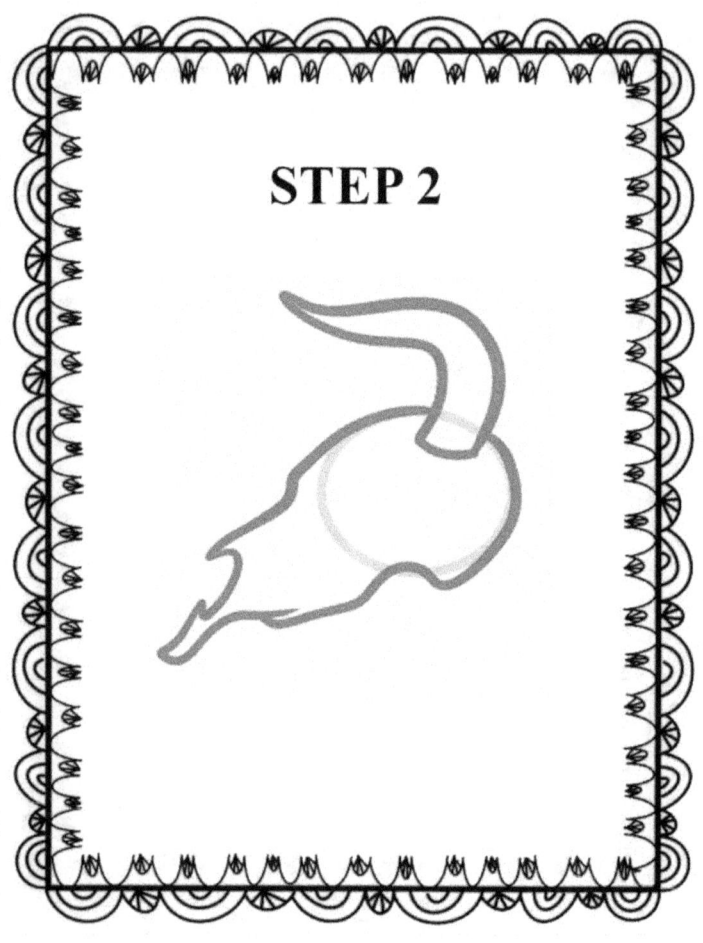

STEP 3

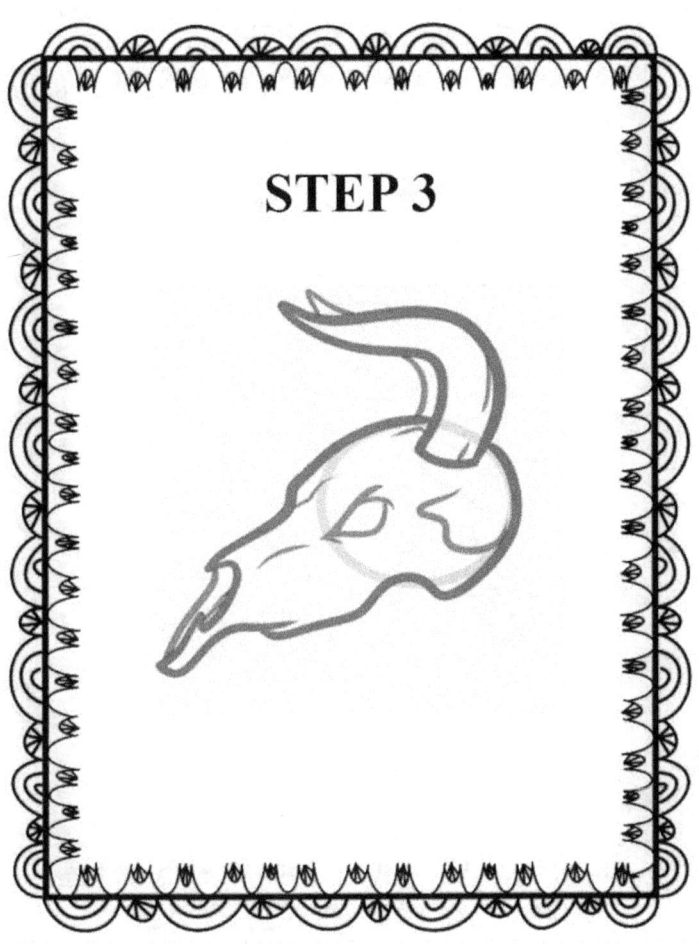

STEP 4

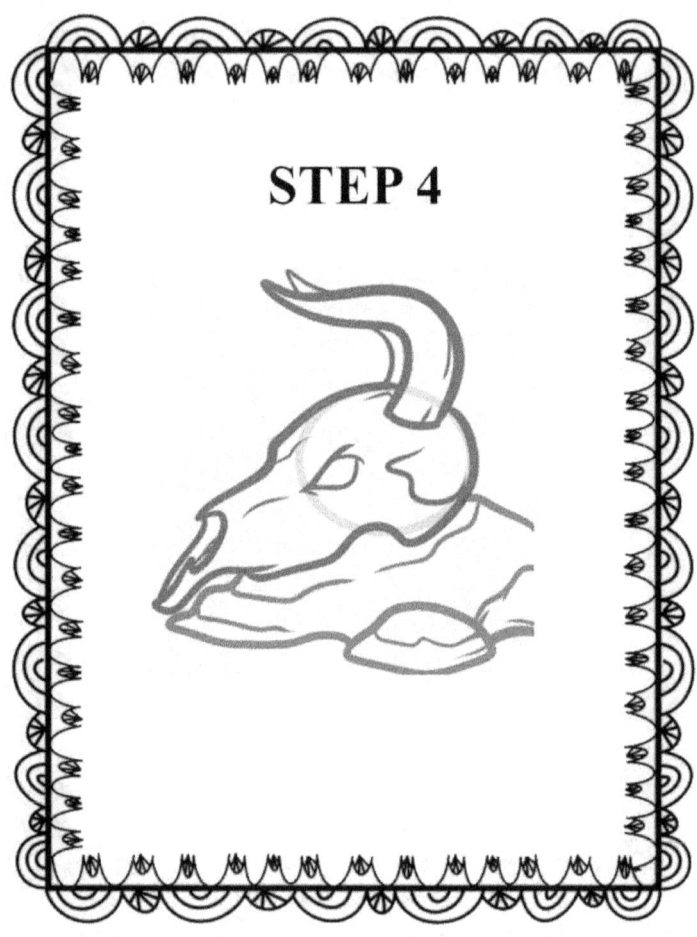

STEP 5

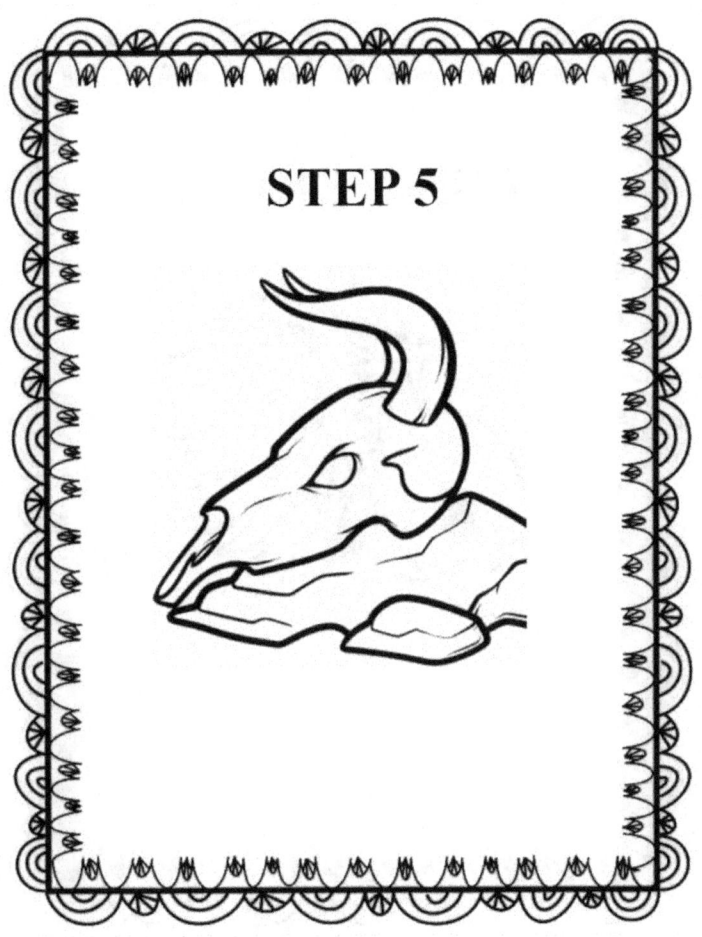

FIERY SKULL

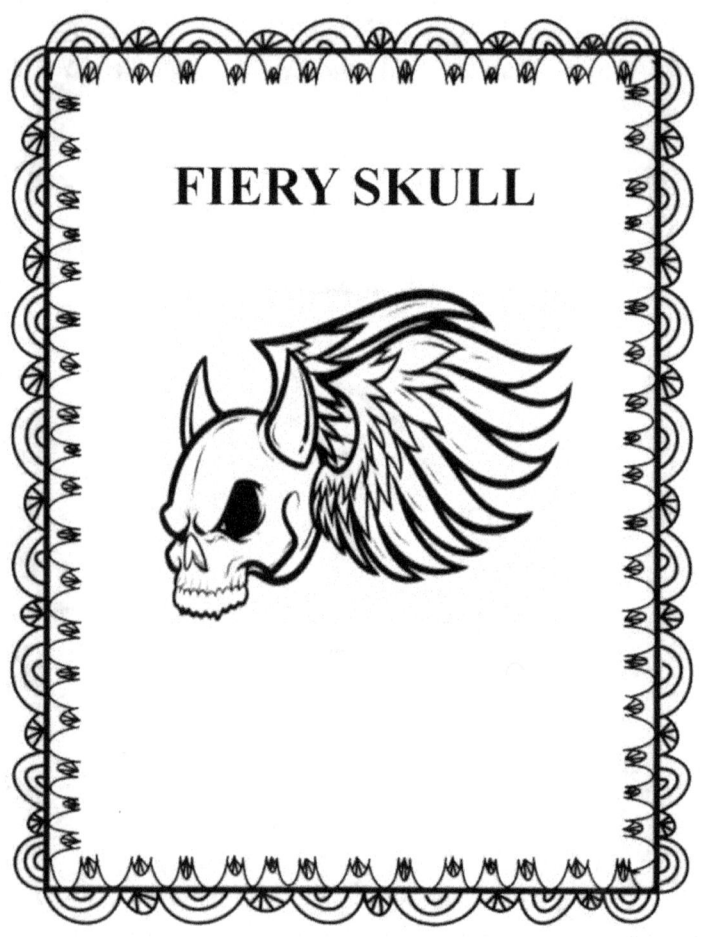

STEP 1

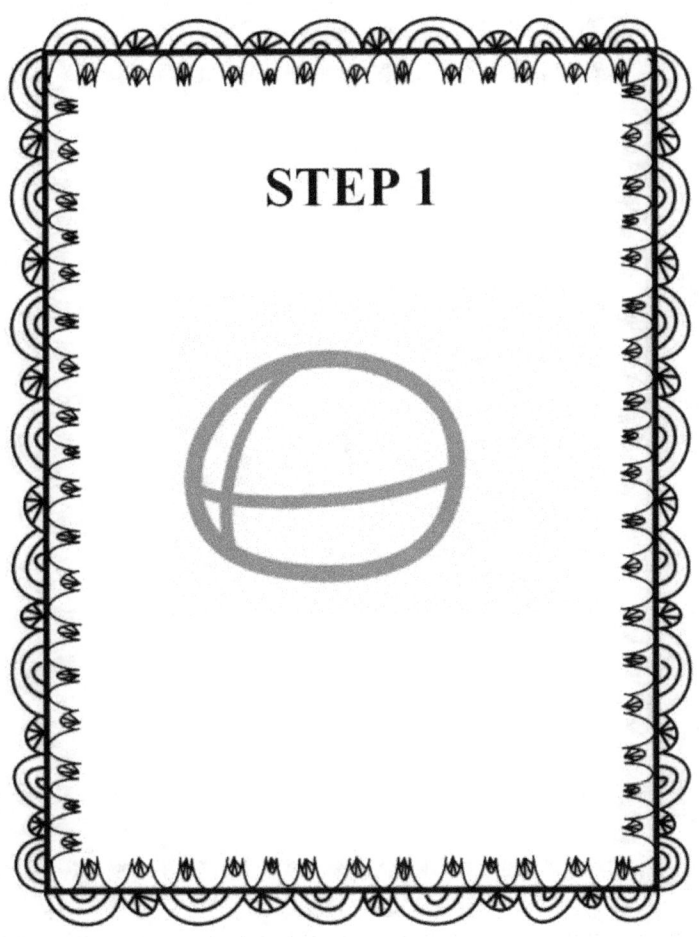

STEP 2

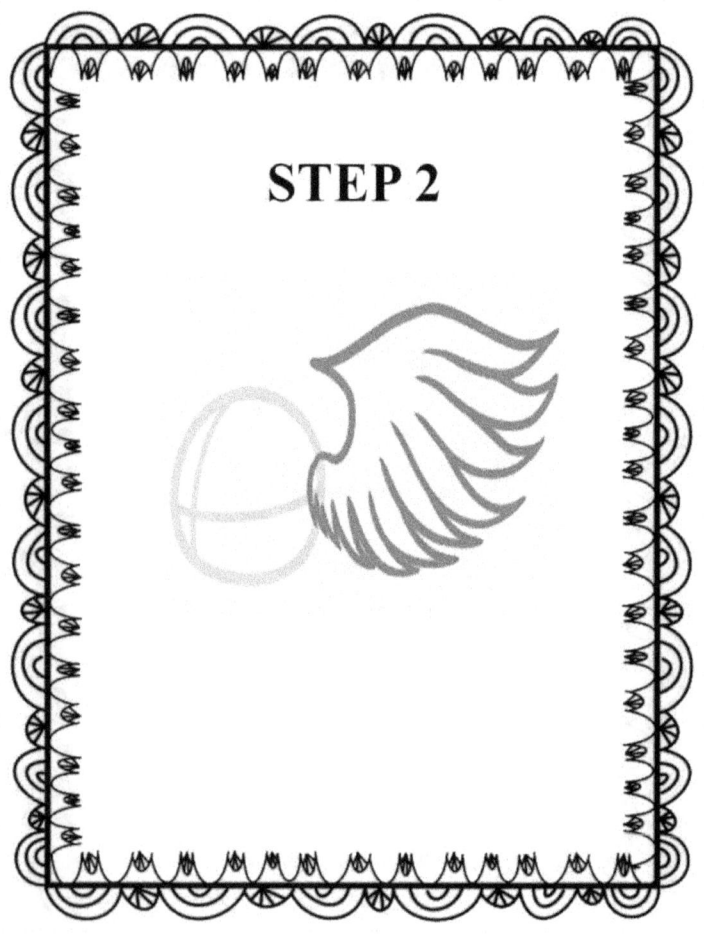

STEP 3

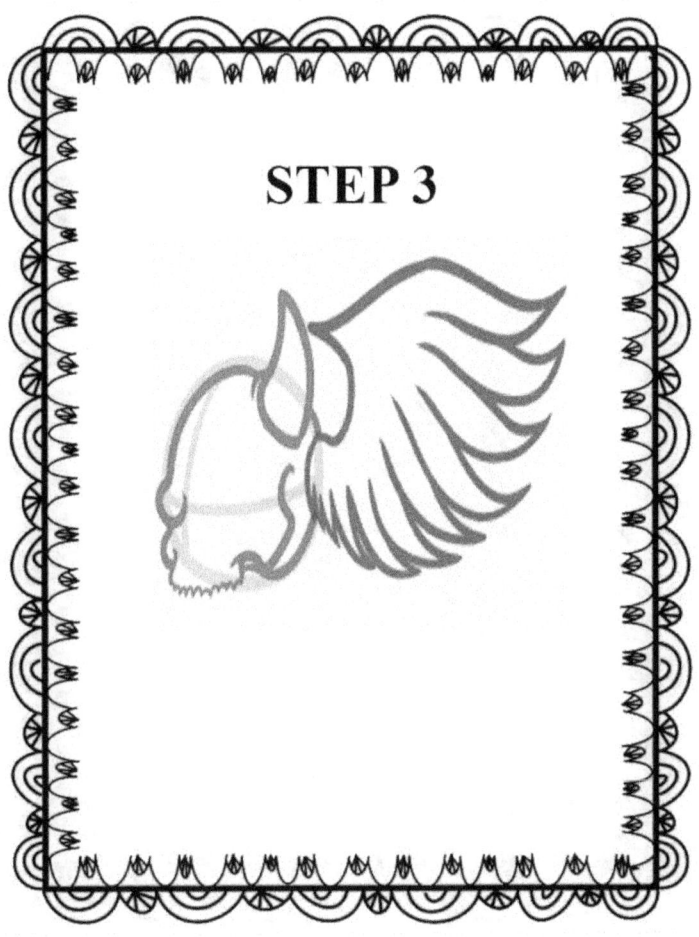

STEP 4

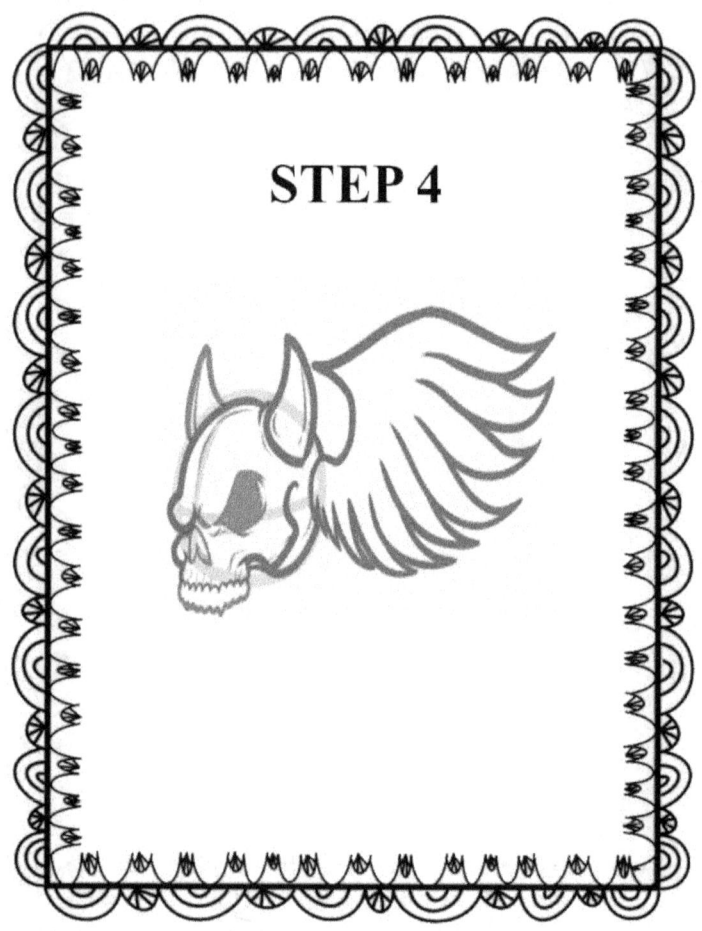

STEP 5

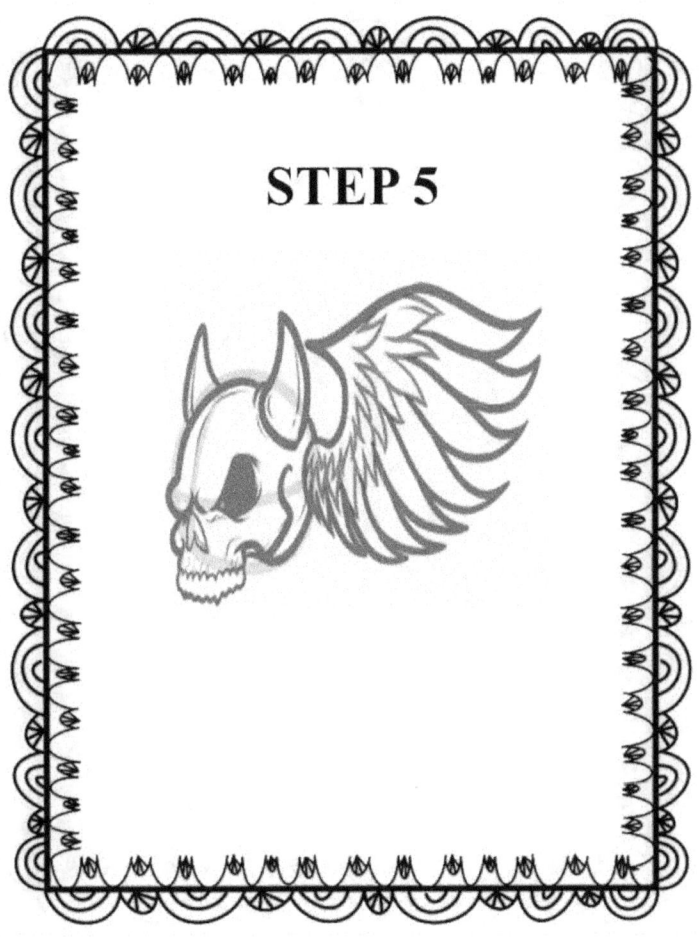

STEP 6

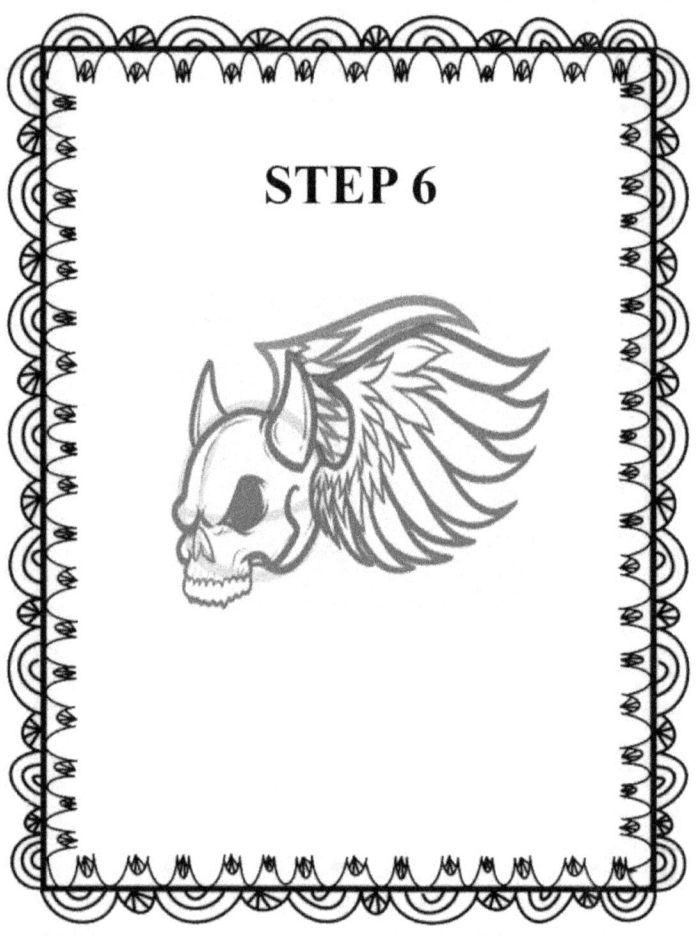

STEP 7

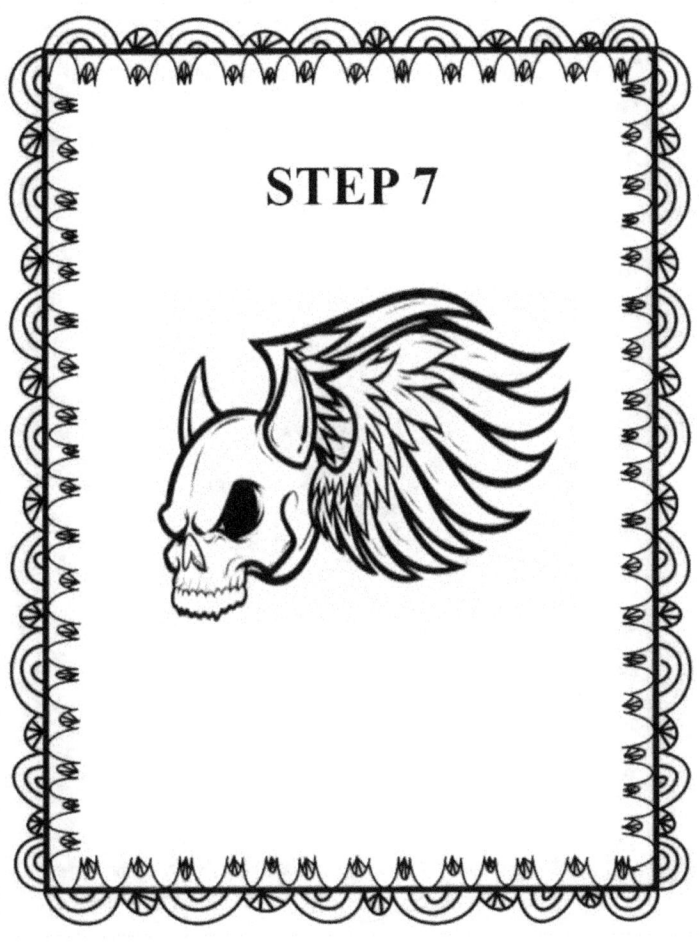

HUMAN SKULL

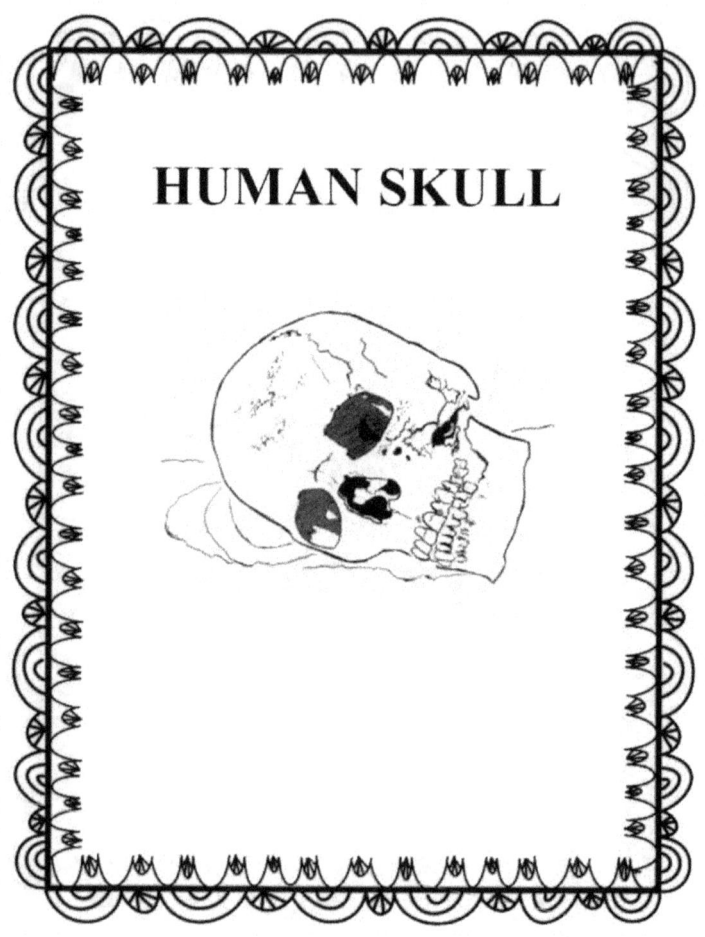

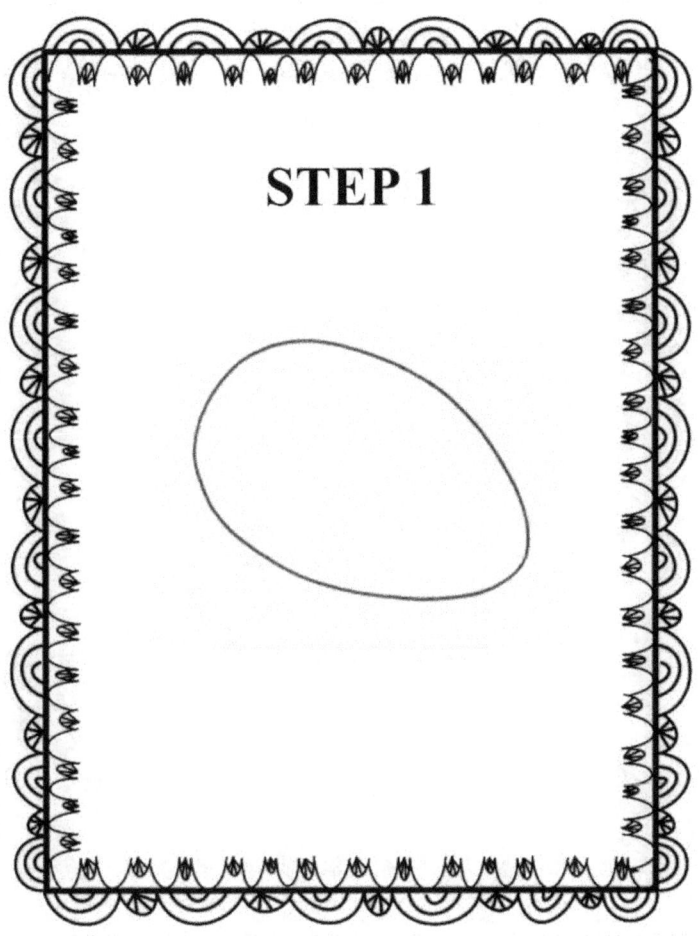

STEP 2

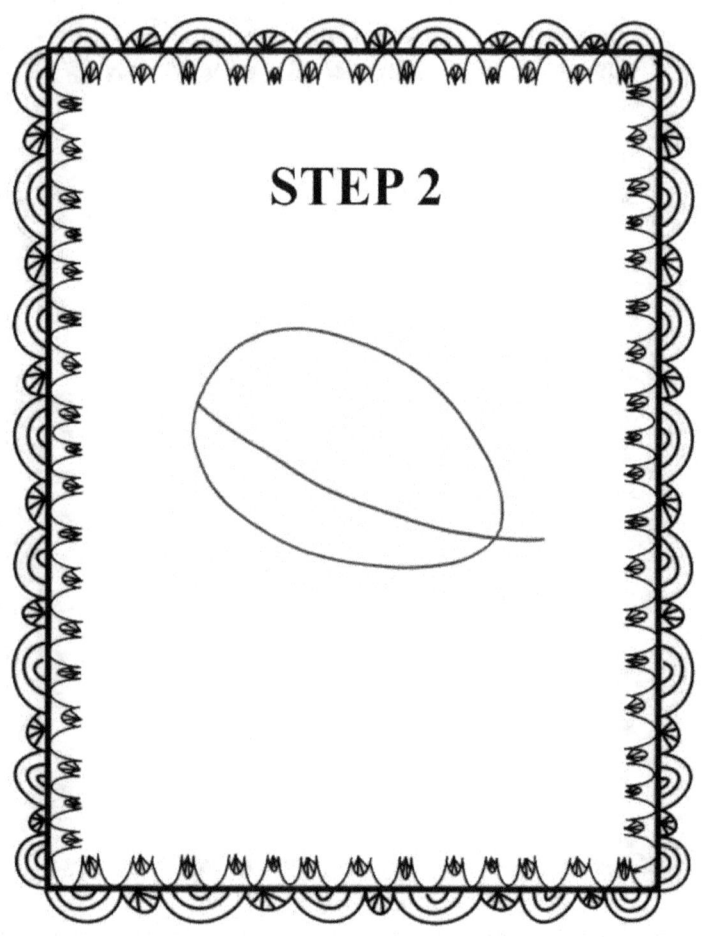

STEP 3

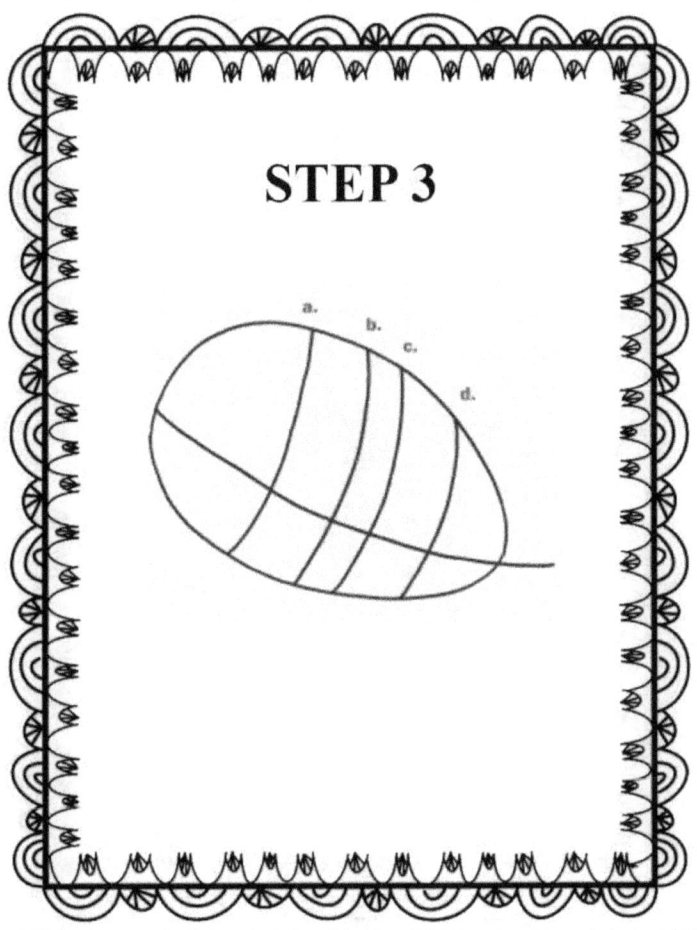

STEP 4

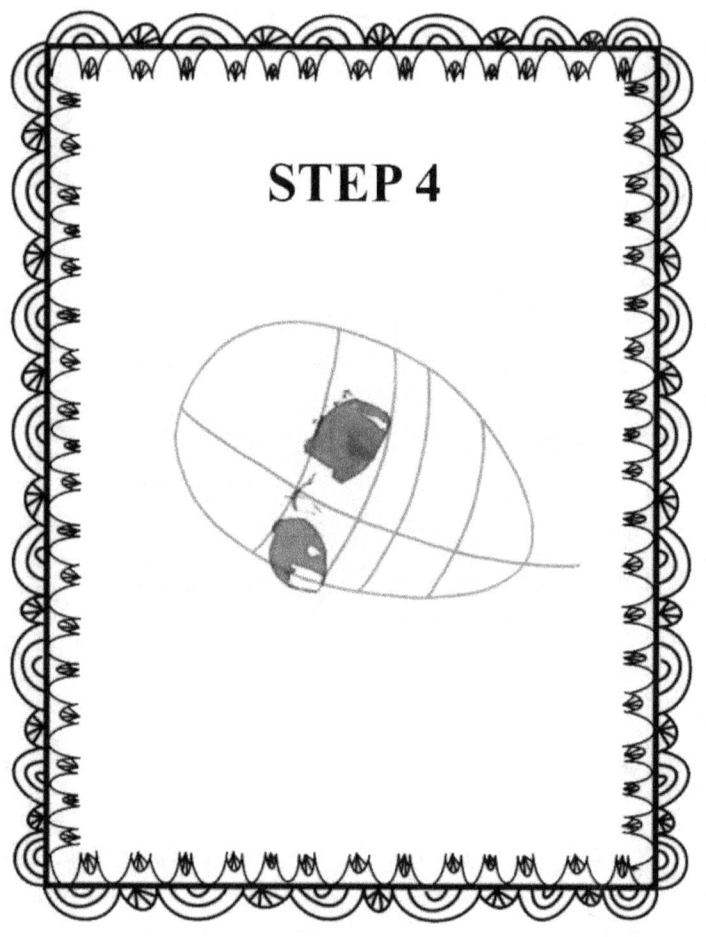

STEP 5

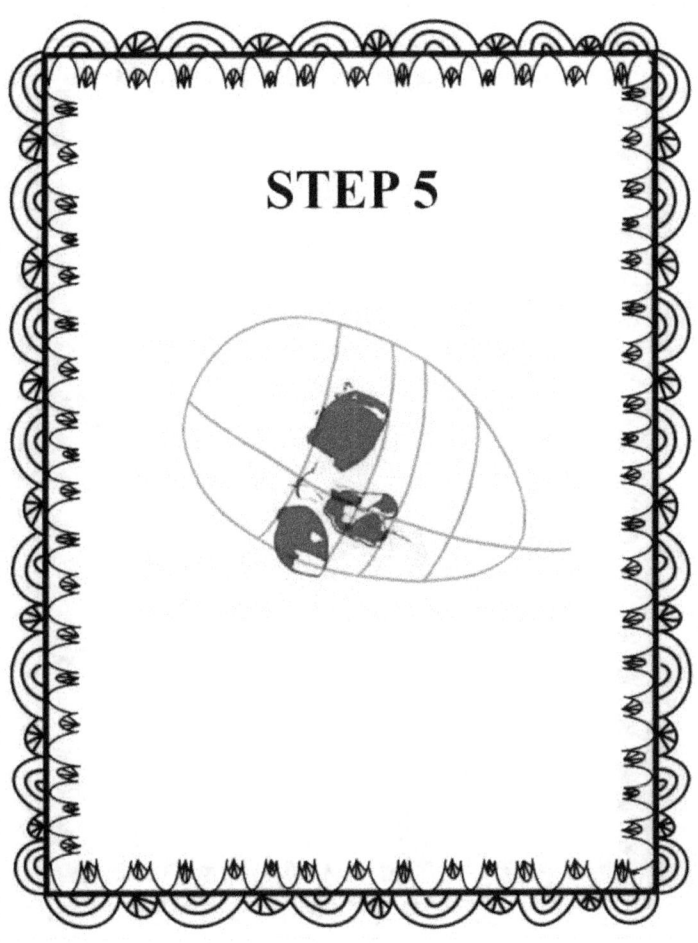

STEP 6

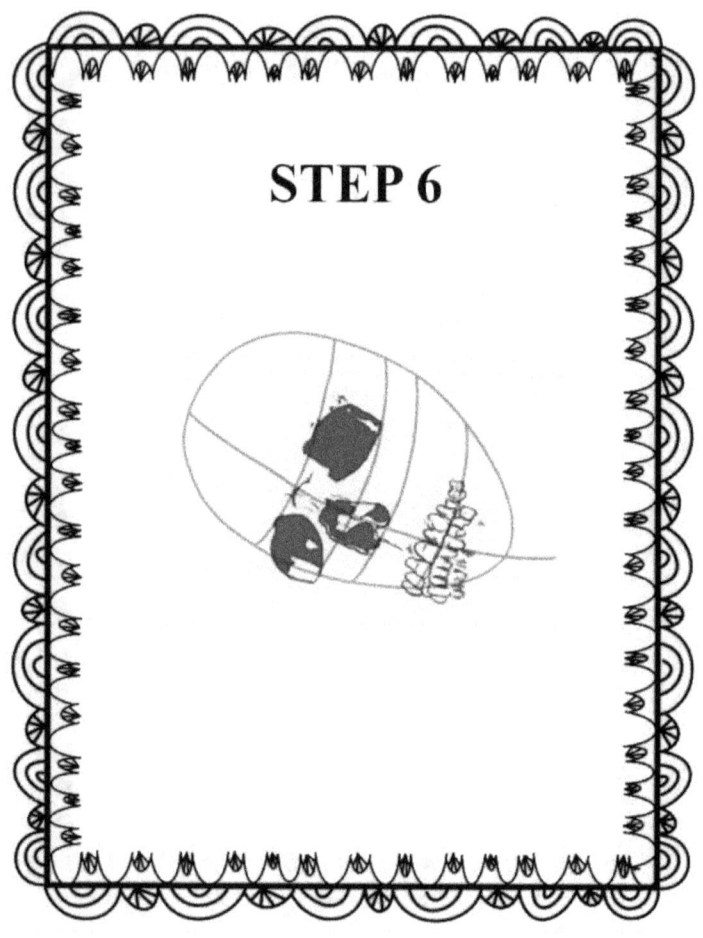

STEP 7

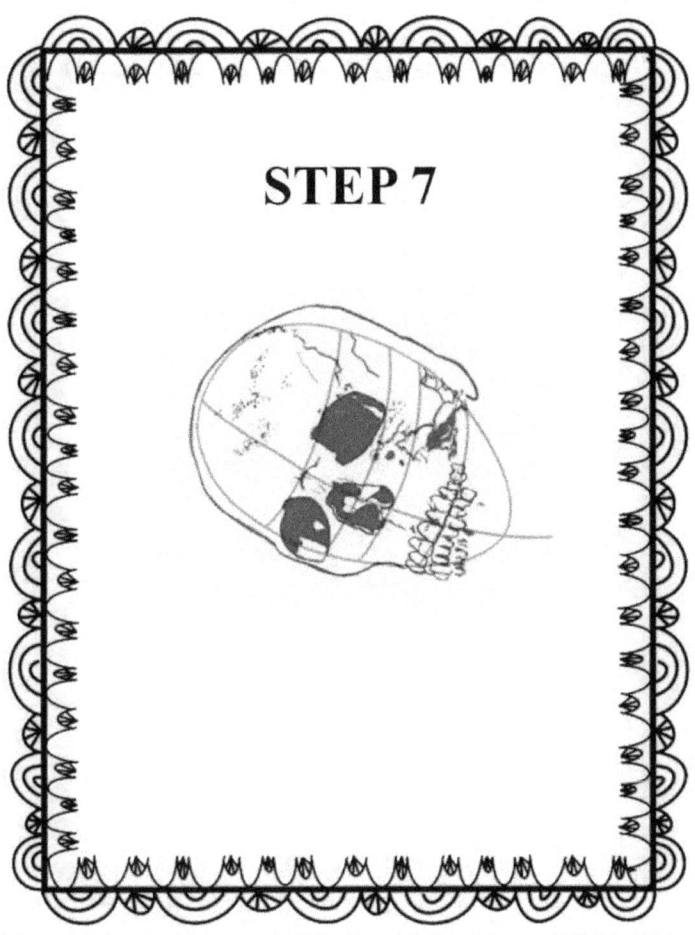

STEP 8

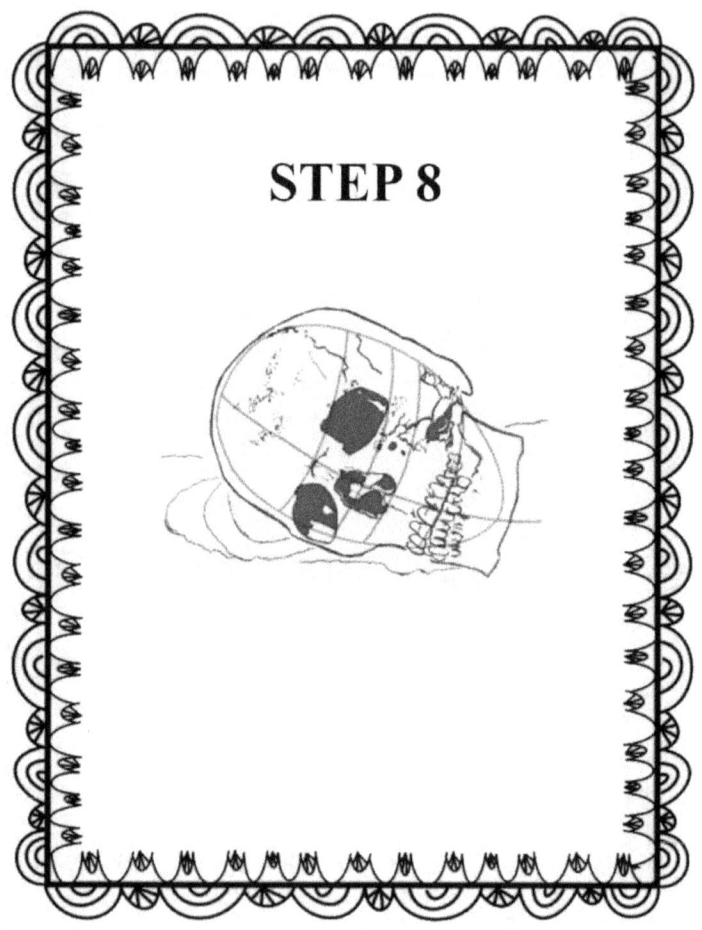

STEP 9

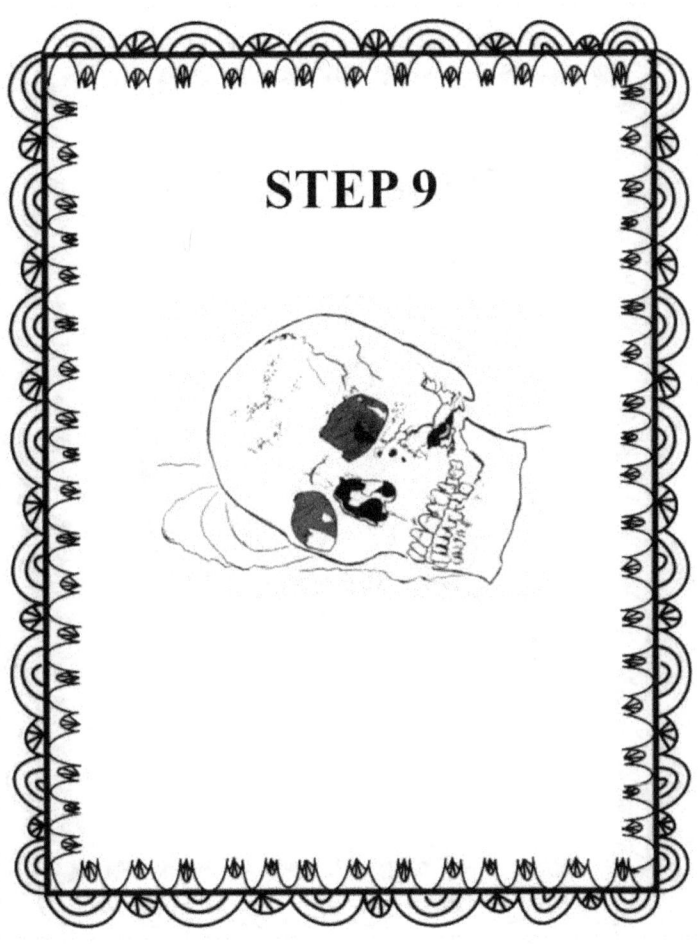

SONICS SKULL

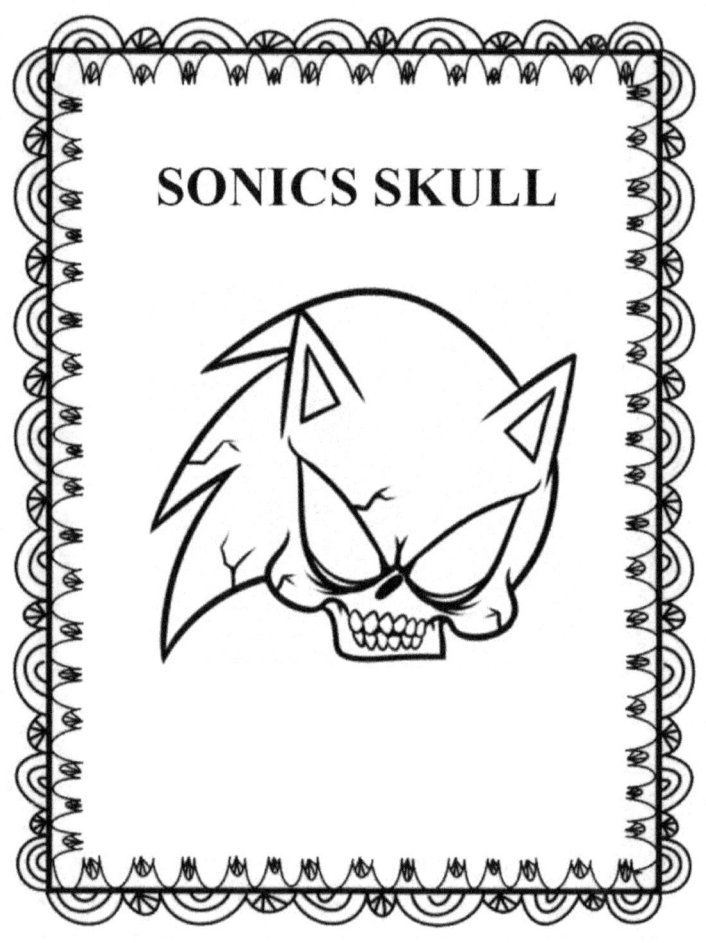

STEP 1

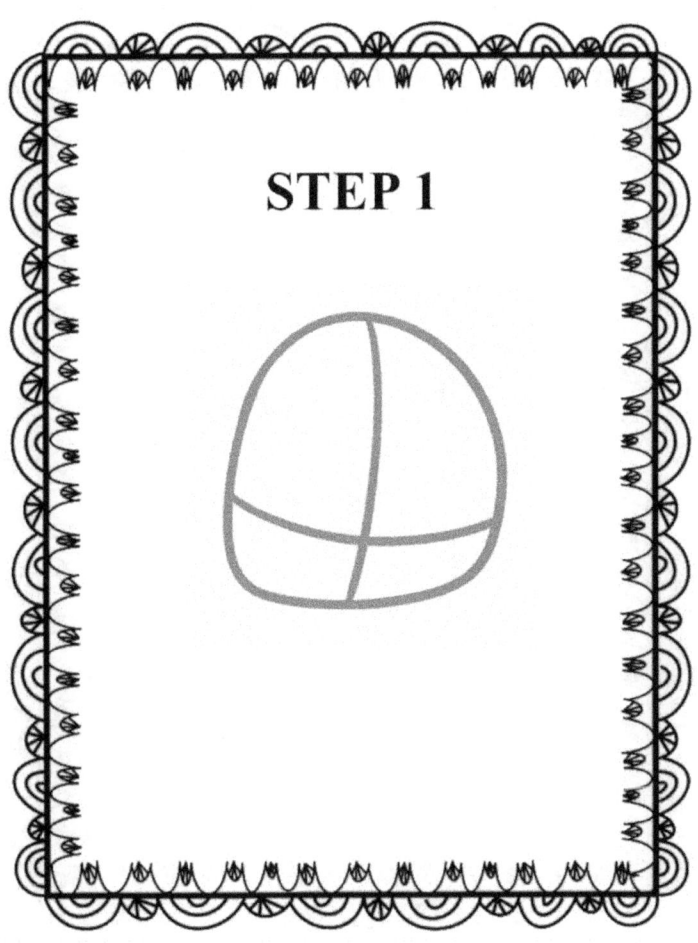

STEP 2

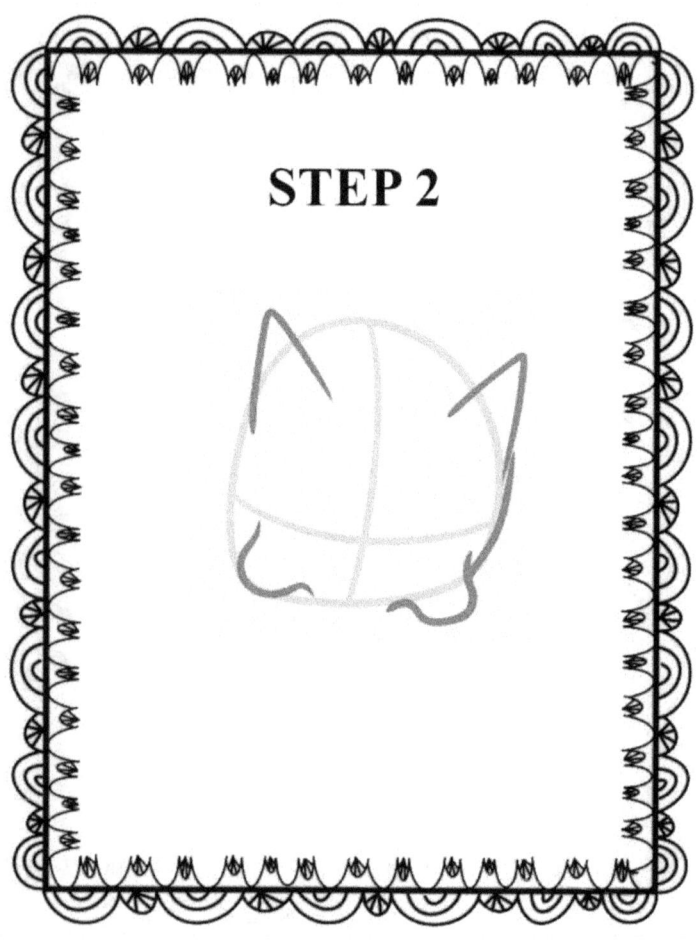

STEP 3

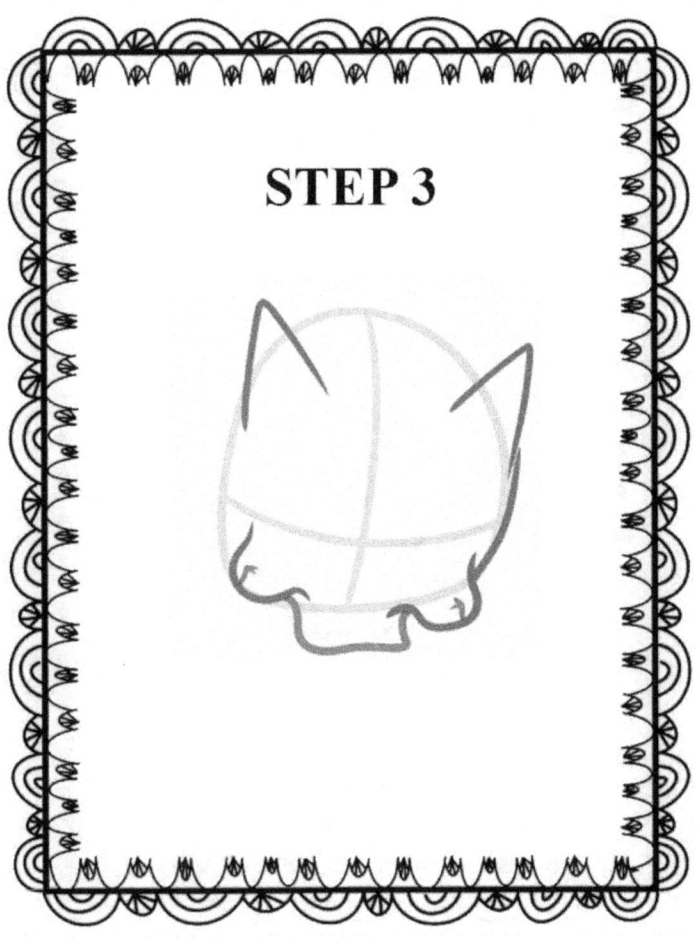

STEP 4

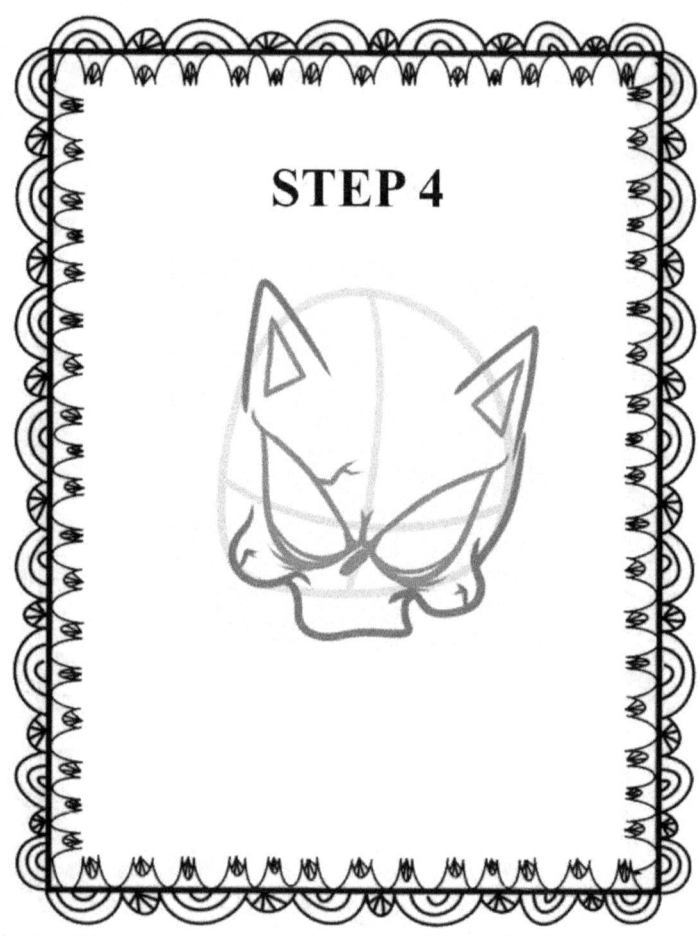

STEP 5

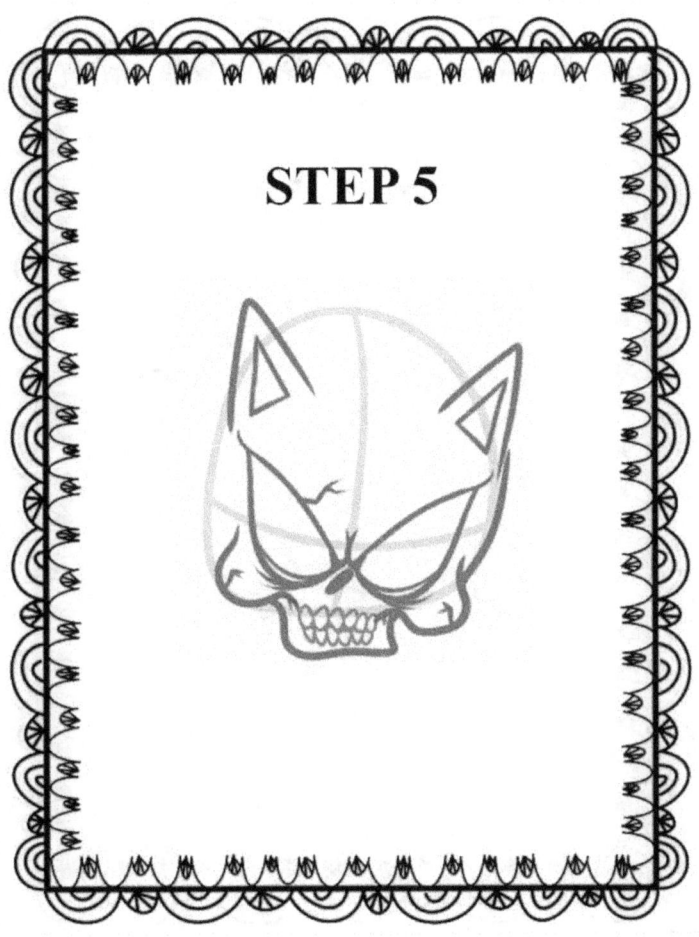

STEP 6

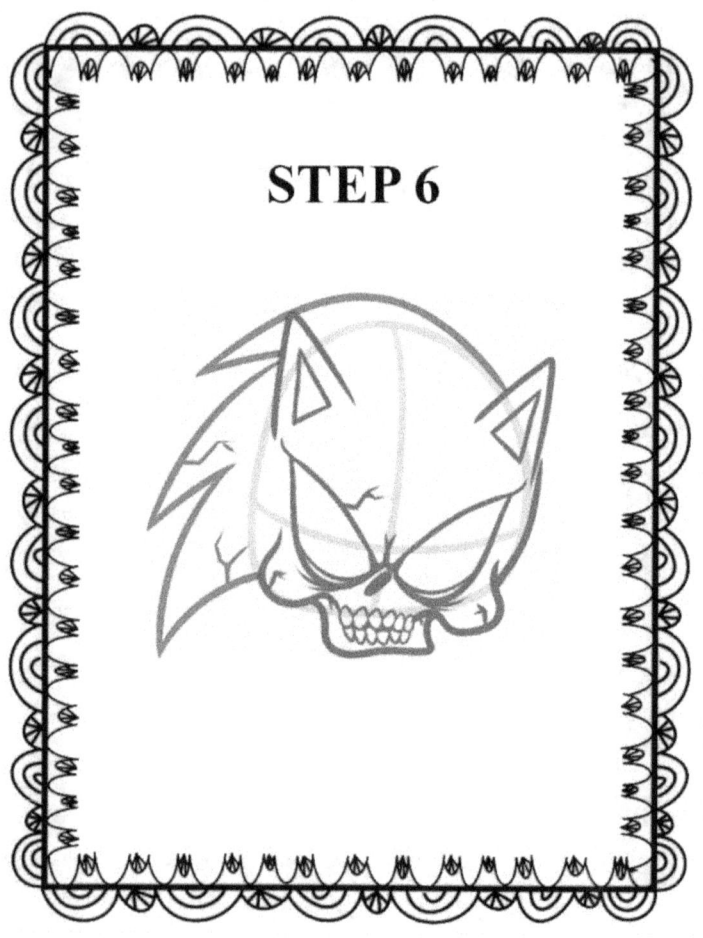

STEP 7

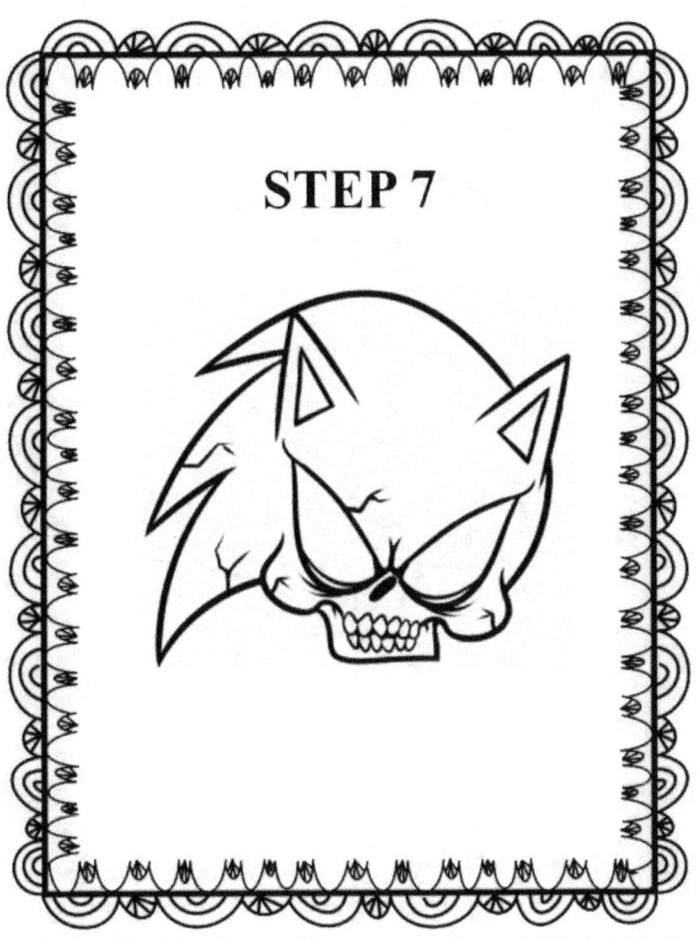

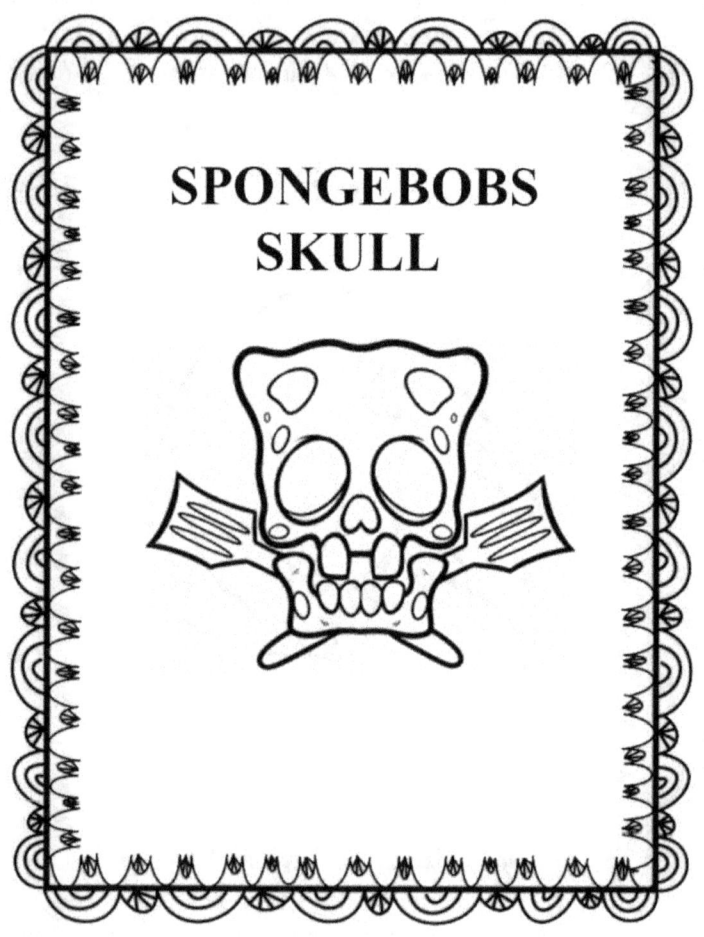

STEP 1

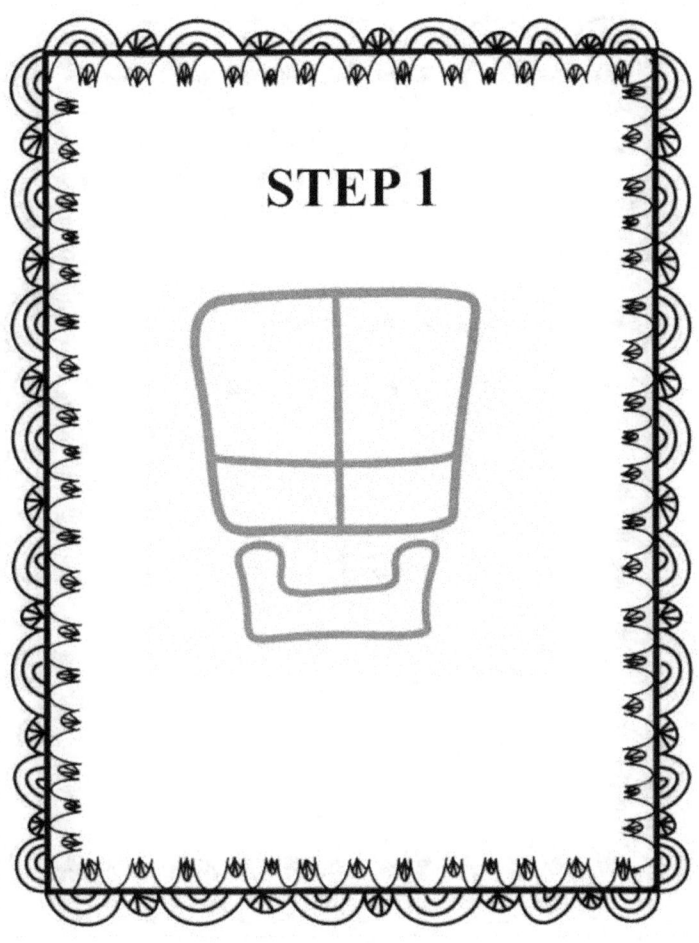

STEP 2

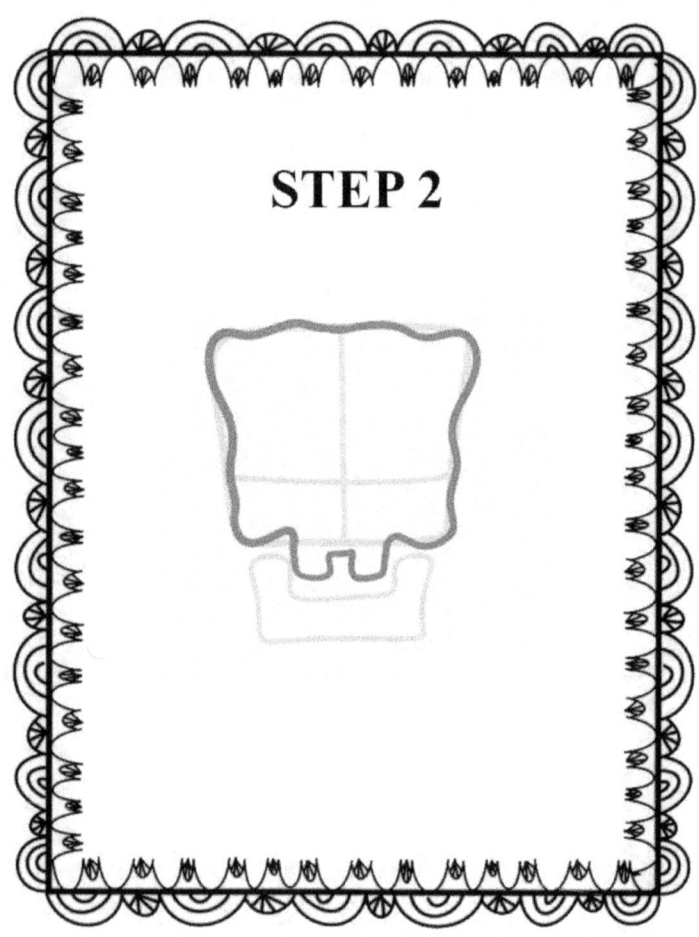

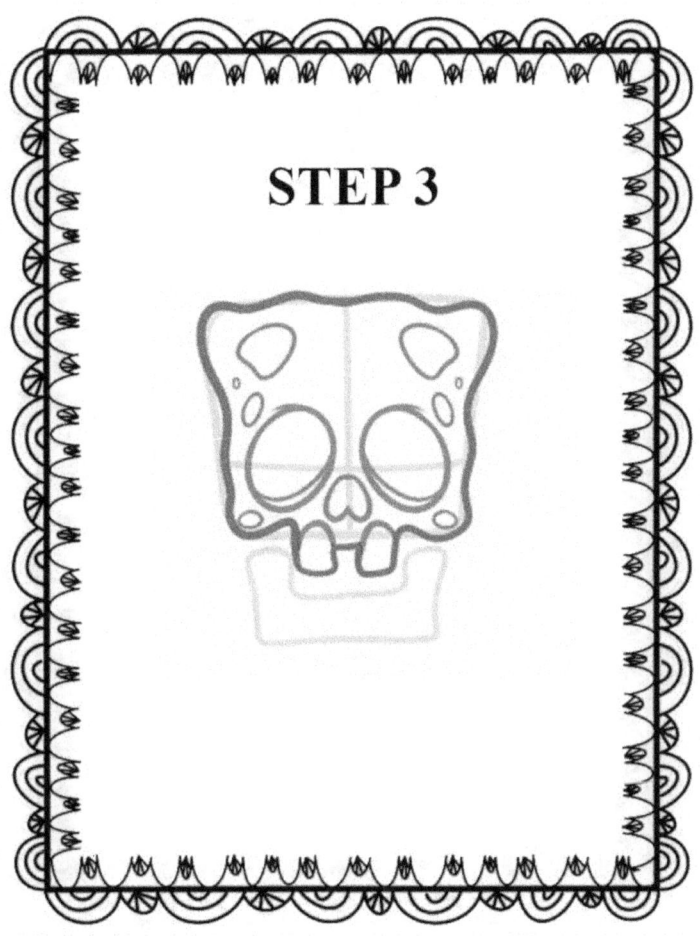

STEP 3

STEP 4

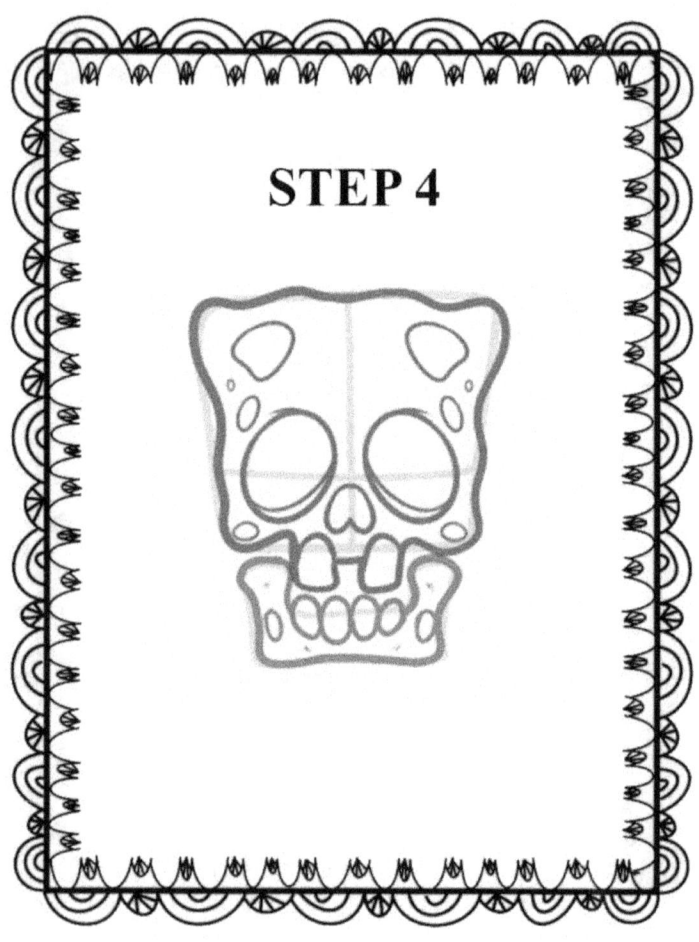

STEP 5

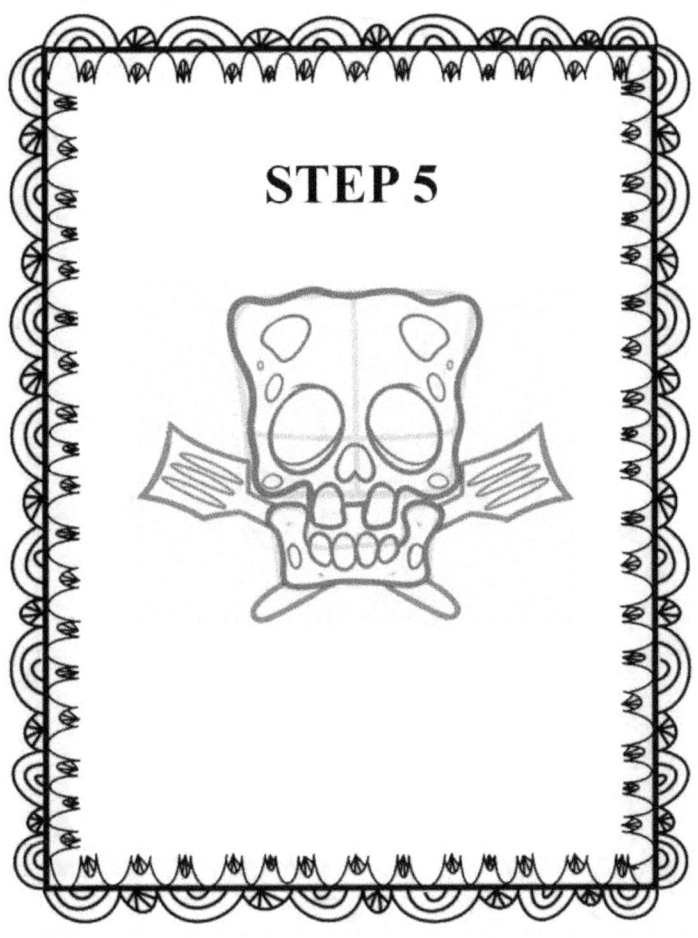

STEP 6

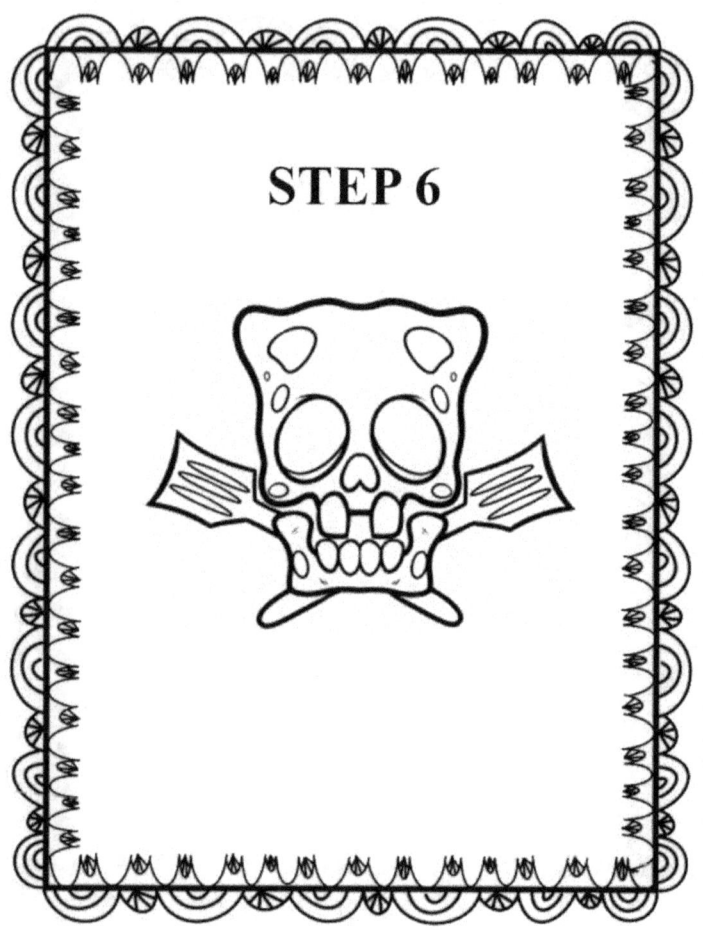

www.ingramcontent.com/pod-product-compliance
Lightning Source LLC
Chambersburg PA
CBHW071644170526
45166CB00003B/1430